Exotic Europeans

THE SOUTH BANK CENTRE

Exhibition Tour

City of Bristol Museum and Art Gallery
19 January - 3 March 1991

Graves Art Gallery, Sheffield
16 March - 28 April

Birmingham Museum and Art Gallery
11 May - 7 July

Walker Art Gallery, Liverpool
24 July - 31 August

A SOUTH BANK CENTRE EXHIBITION

Exhibition organised by Roger Malbert
assisted by Julia Coates

Exhibition design and installation by Frances Vincent

Photographs by:
Chris Dorley-Brown and Marcus Hanson, 3, 4, 6, 7, 11, 12, 14, 15, 19, 20, 21, 25, 26, 27, 30, 31, 32, 35, 36, 37, 38, 39, 47, 48, 54, 55, 57, 88, 89, 90, 91, 103, 104
Werner Forman, 29
Peter Hollings, 44, 50, 51
Matt Squire, 28

Typeset by Quest
Printed in England by Dot-for-Dot Ltd, London

©The South Bank Centre 1991
ISBN 1 85332 066 8

A full list of South Bank Centre publications may be obtained from:
The Publications Office
South Bank Centre, Royal Festival Hall, Belvedere Road, London SE1 8XX

Cover illustration: Ifa Divination Bowl (Cat. 25), photo Chris Dorley-Brown

Contents

Figure of a European
wearing a cap and blazer
Cat. 48

Cultures...Objects...Identities...

CLÉMENTINE DELISS

An Indian, who probably wasn't joking at all, once said: the biggest of all Indian problems is the whiteman. Who can understand the whiteman? What makes him tick? How does he think and why does he think the way he does? Why does he talk so much? Why does he say one thing and do the opposite? Most important of all, how do you deal with him? Obviously, he is here to stay. Sometimes it seems like a hopeless task[1].

There exists a precarious moment in the process of interpretation when ideas previously submerged, still fluid and indeterminate, become recognized and classified. Like argillite, a slate stone only malleable whilst wet, once aired they take on concrete form and express not only a historical moment but, in terms of Western theories of knowledge, a factuality, and a truth value[2].

American Indian conceptions of the "whiteman" during the course of this century became formalized in humour, conveyed through jokes and cultural puns in which imitation offered a source for perpetual critique. The danger of reification, of rendering conceptual models of understanding into rigid stereotypes, was moderated by the indeterminacies of verbal exchange - a joke's success depending on the aptness of its message in the wider context of the conversation. The argillite carvings produced since the 1830s by the Haida Indians of the North West Coast of America were vital items in the trade with European sailors and travellers. Exquisitely carved bas-reliefs on pipes, plates or bowls, they depicted moments in a trade in identities, an exchange of Russian and Haida cultural histories and a recognition of changing traditions. As a medium for communication, these objects could signify the specificity of an encounter: for the Indian by enabling a replication of the totemic sign for export, and for the sailor by allowing him to bring back a souvenir of his travels. When we look at them now, in the context of a museum collection, these moments in art no longer retain the

7

transience of interpretations but all too often their meanings have become solidified and validated by a Western system of classification.

The "scientific" nomenclature which we have established around objects, coupling materiality with the written word, needs to be viewed with a certain apprehension. For not only does it indicate our engrained fear of the indeterminate, of interpretations which remain loose and malleable, but it can stifle the potential for new constructions of cultural identity which are negotiated and include a recasting of historical "truths".

Exotic Europeans brings together over one hundred sculptures, paintings and artefacts from Africa, Asia, the Far East and the Americas. Within the cultural and temporal diversity of these objects there lies a common theme: contact with the European and a European identity. A bamboo pole from New Caledonia traditionally used to depict scenes of local life and indigenous cosmology, displays intricate engravings of men, some brandishing axes, others, most likely to be French colonial administrators, holding rifles and dressed in breeches and pith helmets. A late nineteenth-century Company painting from India shows two Europeans riding high on elephants and supervising a tiger shoot. When they are not engaged in armed conflict, Europeans are seen transported in palanquins, seated on stools drinking gin and comandeering, or otherwise involved in lascivious activity with courtesans. No detail is overlooked, from the neatly parted hair and upturned moustache of the French colonial in Mexico, to the stern expression of the British administrator in East Africa. Facial characteristics, indications of mood, styles of uniform and body posture make these depictions of Europeans both highly entertaining and acutely satirical. Each representation, however, displays the identity of the outsider seen through the eyes of the indigenous artist. In this sense we are only able to recognize that which we know to be ourselves and it is here that the problems of interpretation begin. The Europeans we see in this exhibition are exotic: they introduce an outside vision into a familiar arena and in so doing they inevitably encourage us to re-qualify our stereotypical construction of the past.

Visual depictions of Europeans by non-Western cultures constitute a maverick category in the West's various art historical disciplines. They do not affirm our presuppositions of the "authentic" Other, the "traditional" society, untainted by foreign contact, but have been viewed ambiguously as the uncomfortable evidence of our obsession with expansionist forms of economic and political power and our zeal for the cultural and spiritual reformation of other peoples. The artefacts on view in *Exotic Europeans* were brought together from the numerous collections of non-Western art in the United Kingdom. More often regarded as miscellaneous art objects, they were collected nonetheless by traders, explorers and anthropologists over the course of the last three hundred years. Housed in "museums of mankind", they speak of a crossing of cultures, conveying certain moments, certain conditions, which in retrospect become increasingly difficult to determine.

The ethnographic museum, for example, epitomizes a later stage in European expansion, and a period during which the economic and political subjugation of other cultures went hand in hand with an academic analysis of their cultural forms. This implies that whatever the origins of the object may be, once it is contained within this early twentieth-century institution, it acquires a classificatory tag which ties it to a later form of colonialist intervention. Most objects removed from their country of origin have only one date: the date of collection, and very often even this record is lost. The pillaging of Africa's traditional art forms by the West during the course of the late nineteenth and early twentieth centuries has enforced an amnesia upon Africa's own past. Histories need to be rebuilt and museums have as their duty to encourage this process to take place. A survey such as *Exotic Europeans* suggests that if there have been several periods in European exploration, so too have there been several types of "stranger", ranging from the more to the less benign.

The first period of contact with the "outside world" was initiated by the Portuguese in the mid-fifteenth century. Keen to crack the Venetian monopoly on luxury items from the East, the Portuguese set up trading relationships with the various rulers along the West coast of Africa. In exchange for pepper, elephant teeth and tusks, amber and indigo, the Africans received coloured cottons and silks, coral and Venetian glass beads, hats and caps, coats of mail, mirrors and drinking glasses. This mercantile potential was soon to benefit the British and the French who, by the early sixteenth century, had reached the African shores together with their European brothers, the Danes, Swedes and Germans. During the course of the fifteenth and sixteenth centuries European explorers made contact with the Americas (1492), Southern China (1516), New Guinea (1526), Japan (1542) and New Zealand (1642). The presence of these intruders was to lead to a revision of the indigenous concept of the "stranger" as a person who, to take the Akan example from Ghana, was internal to the culture but identified as being outside of the local political and kinship community[3].

Representations of the new foreigners from this early stage are rare but can be found on well-preserved Indian miniatures, on fifteenth-century Afro-Portuguese ivories carved in Sierra Leone for export to Portuguese royal courts, and on the bronze plaques depicting Portuguese soldiers which once lined the Oba of Benin's palace. These bronze casts, unlike wooden carvings which are so susceptible to climactic conditions, have survived hundreds of years and are now widely considered to be among the finest examples of African art known. Sadly no longer decorating the walls of the palace, they have been forcibly removed from their original site. Their context, like so much of the visual histories of non-Western societies, has been relocated within the confines of the museum and re-contextualized within the Western framework of cultural values.

The second period in European expansionism no longer carried with it the relatively benign implications of mercantile trade. From the sixteenth century right through to the mid-nineteeth century slave traffic, alongside gold, dominated European interests in the Other, and in Africa in particular. Depictions of slave raids can be found on Loango carved ivory tusks and very often a gin-drinking European slave trader will feature in the role of the proto-typical 'foreigner' - now no longer a partner in trade but unhealthily encroaching on the totality of the African existence. The main monuments to the European presence during this period are both too large and too ambivalent for any collector. The slave fortresses of Cape Coast and Elmina in Ghana (the Gold Coast of British Colonial Rule) are examples of European fifteenth to sixteenth century architecture constructed primarily from imported bricks and timber transported to Africa on returning slave ships. They loom large, white and empty, allowing today's visitor to wander through the officers' mess right down to the dungeons below, damp and reeking of the darkness Europeans projected onto the African continent.

With the abolition of the slave trade in the latter half of the nineteenth century, the object of European interest shifted from an ownership of human labour to one of land and raw materials. By 1912, Europeans had colonized the whole of the African continent except for Ethiopia and Liberia. When the First World War broke out, African colonies were divided up between the British, French, Germans, Italians, Spaniards, Portuguese and Belgians. The British alone had control over nearly half a million square miles. Myths were propagated by white politicians in order to legitimize the European presence. In South Africa it was falsely said that when van Riebeeck landed in the Cape, Bantu speaking peoples were only just crossing the Limpopo and that the land was therefore empty. The prior presence of indigenous cultures was barely acknowledged, leading to a disavowal of African culture and a legitimation of White supremacist ideology[4].

The complex modalities of colonial rule necessitated an ever-growing number of functionaries and administrators. 'Strangers' in colonial societies included intermediaries such as civil service bureaucrats and clerks, entrepreneurs, small independent businessmen, and entrenched Europeans such as district officers, technical advisors, teachers and missionaries. In India, the European merged into the internal political structure without resorting to quite the extremism and degree of brutal subjugation exercized in Africa. Although, in principle, trade control lay in the hands of the Indians, the British were still able to manipulate its course and take charge of Indian administration.

Whether it was to Africa, Asia or the Far East, Europeans were globe-trotting like never before, keen to educate and reform, to carry out the humanistic precepts of the eighteenth century and, above all, to control and collect. Representations of Europeans in paintings and carvings from this later period are far more widespread in museums in the West and are therefore relatively straightforward to locate. Colonialism grew hand in hand with the anthropological study of other cultures, and in several European states, such as France and Germany, this interest was directly linked to the collection and investigation of material artefacts.

In 1878, E.T. Hamy, a doctor trained under the psychiatrist Charcot, founded the Musée d'Ethnographie du Trocadero (now Musée de l' Homme) in Paris. The Musée was established in contradistinction to earlier curiosity cabinets and was specifically concerned with the classification of material culture. Indeed it was through an analysis of mainly functional artefacts that anthropologists believed they could reach the depths of 'native' culture. The working hypothesis that a society or culture could be analysed primarily through its objects remained the basis for a large proportion of anthropological studies right through until the Second World War. Major expeditions were launched such as the Mission Dakar Djibouti, which crossed Africa in 1931-33, and brought a booty back to Paris of over 3,500 artefacts, including 60 m² of sixteenth century Abyssinian murals peeled off the walls of the church of St Antonios in Gondar, Ethiopia[5]. Although the British were less systematic than the French in collecting 'ethnographic' objects for data, it was during this later period (mid nineteenth to early twentieth centuries) that museums in the United Kingdom acquired the majority of their present collections.

In general, the emphasis lay on objects which appeared to represent 'traditional' belief systems and social structures untainted by contact with the West. Carvings which depicted the outside world in terms of a European whiteman were only gradually recognized by some as constituting important visual records of the course of history.

In 1937, Julius Lips wrote the first comprehensive account documenting the visual representations of Europeans in non-Western cultures. He believed that in the absence of a written history[6], these visual expressions actually constituted a powerful and satirical indigenous voice, a sign of rebellion against the white oppressor. Lips was a German refugee from Nazi Germany and was sensitive to issues of racism. His idiosyncratic work uses this particular category in the arts of non-Western peoples as a vehicle to condemn the intolerance and inhumanity of Hitler's regime. In spite of certain eccentricities in Lips theory, *The Savage Hits Back* offers a useful typology of European 'strangers' and their identity as seen through the sculptures and paintings of Africa, Asia, and the Far East. He covers the main icons of European contact, ranging from the sailing ship to the generic 'whiteman' portrayed in his different functions and occasionally accompanied by a stern wife. Indeed there is a marked absence of imagery of the white woman, who in terms of power clearly took a secondary position. Few women were prepared to travel to the 'White Man's Grave' whether it be in Sierra Leone or the Far East. Those who have been depicted, are presented as austere of character and faith, active in running the colonial household or in preaching the mission. The numerous objects which help to qualify the European identity include guns, chairs, musical instruments, padlocks, keys, pipes, hats, pith helmets, tableware, watches, bicycles and motor cars. Lips also refers to the 'chieftains of the whites': the momentous figures of Edward VII, Wilhelm II and of course Queen Victoria. Made in replica of the official bust portrait which circulated on stamps, magazines and photographs, the Yoruba carvings of the Queen end rather abruptly below the bosom in two small, comical legs shrouded by the costume of the period. Emblems, heraldic signets and the Union Jack are also popular icons of foreign power and can be traced on the appliquéd flags of Ghanaian Fante Asafo military institutions.

The European identity represented in the form of carvings, paintings and various functional artefacts such as pipes, walking sticks and export porcelain ware (China) became of commercial interest for the West at two separate phases in the marketing of non-Western art. The first was motivated by a sentimental and romanticizing desire to acquire a souvenir of one's travels. These early forms of Europeanized representation acted in many ways as a confirmation of the beneficial nature of expansionism. When icons of Western 'civilization' and Christian religious belief were discovered in the crafts of peoples pejoratively defined as 'primitive', the justification for reformatory action was in itself confirmed. However, these objects, exchanged between sailors and the local people or commissioned by royal courts, were treated nonetheless as mere curiosities. The emphasis on the 'art' dimension was not yet fully exploited.

From the late 1960s onwards, the interest in objects which conveyed explicit signs of cultural contact became firmly established. Lips' early survey of the 'whiteman' in the visual arts of non-European peoples has itself become a collector's item and has formed the basis for subsequent art-histories. Cottie Burland's *The Exotic White Man* published in Britain in 1969 is a review of four centuries of art, an art which in his words conveys "the impact on the soul of this contact with another person from a distant land"[7]. Purged of the Lipsian fervour to grant the 'native' the benefit of an acute and biting satirical voice, Burland's patronizing descriptions of the objects and the contexts in which they were produced makes uncomfortable reading for anyone with an ounce of critical judgement. Moreover, what this type of globalizing art-history suggests is that there was very little attempt as yet to interpret the reasons for the continuing use of the European identity in iconographic form within the various non-Western cultures.

Nearly fifty years after the publication of *The Savage Hits Back*, a German collector of African art, Jens Jahn, organized an exhibition of what he termed 'Colon' art. Making a pun on the 'colonization' of the African art market itself, Jahn grouped together African carvings from the late 19th and early 20th centuries. The common theme was the European, ranging from the stereotypical soldier to the district officer and the missionary.

For Jahn 'Colon' art has to be understood as more than just an aesthetic style. It provides a category within the African arts which is not strictly purist and does not search for an 'authentic' or 'traditional' iconography. Instead 'Colon' art can be viewed as an important visual record of colonial intervention. Although Lips emphasizes the satirical and implicitly anti-imperialist content of the artefacts, Jahn claims he does not attempt to understand the role these objects play within the very culture which produces them. Jahn's interest in the representation of Europeans in Africa has led historians and anthropologists to develop more elaborate theories around these testimonies of colonial contact.

Edward Graham-Norris, a contributor to the Jahn catalogue, suggests that 'Colon' objects do not exist in order to create an outside dialogue with the 'whiteman' but find their meaning within the society and culture of the artist who actually makes them[8]. In other words, these artefacts are created in order to help people negotiate amongst themselves an identity around a totally new concept of the Other, in this case, arising out of the imposition of colonial rule. For Norris, 'Colon' sculptures reflect a superficial transformation of traditional forms and he offers three separate models for understanding and interpreting this art-form.

Following Levi-Strauss, the first interpretation suggests that 'Colon' is nothing more than the random use of a current sign or icon to express and communicate a more fundamental issue. The meaning below the superficial transformation does not alter. The particular iconography is chosen arbitrarily and may or may not correspond with the events of the moment. The second interpretation suggests that in fact the signifier (e.g. a Yoruba representation of Queen Victoria) is inherently related to the social reality which surrounds it (e.g. Victorian imperialism). 'Colon' carvings are therefore direct attempts to illustrate these new realities. Finally, following a Freudian psychoanalytical concept of trauma, 'Colon' can be understood as a cathartic attempt to come to terms with colonisation and the disruption of indigenous social and religious norms. This third interpretation, however seductive to the Western mind, presupposes a notion of therapeutic agency which may not necessarily be compatible with indigenous models of healing. It should be added that the popularity of Jahn's exhibition and its informative publication has had major repercussions in West Africa, and dealers there are busily 'discovering' large quantities of such objects in their back-yard with Jahn's book on *Colon Kunst* acting as a guideline.

All these various explanatory models indicate the problem of generalizing on the meaning and function of these images of Europeans. If they are, each in their manner, attempts to negotiate a reality by transfering this recognition of change onto an iconographic medium, then we must not only look at the specificity of their own cultural expression, but accept the possibility of variations in meaning. In other words, we in the West who have ruthlessly collected these objects cannot provide the 'true' interpretation of them. How we see them, understand them and classify them is not how they were intended to be viewed and interpreted in the first instance. The objects illustrate different moments in the historical perceptions of people who were subjected at various times and in various forms to European culture and identity. Rather than accept one interpretation for them it seems wiser to take several into account, thereby suspending the notion of a single validating rationalization which amounts to the 'real' reason for their existence. It then becomes possible to view these objects as participatory elements in a trade of identities. A label which tries to describe the object on show is nothing more nor less than a further attempt at contextualization. It cannot determine the meaning of the object anymore than an object can in essence offer a single and static notion of cultural identity.

Exhibitions are sites for thought, for ideas inspired by the objects on display. By intermingling different cultural systems into a single exhibition space one hopes to encourage the visitor to create his or her own personal context around the artefacts. *Exotic Europeans* is therefore an exhibition about the various ways in which very different cultures and societies have set about interpreting the impact of the European upon their understanding of the world. No exhibition can claim to be comprehensive and cover all moments and expressions of a chosen subject. The exhibits here were selected both on the grounds of their wit and aesthetic appeal, and because they convey, each in their manner, a very strong image of contact seen not through our eyes but expressed through the history-making processes of other cultures. The exhibits have been presented in a heterogeneous manner in order to highlight the differences and the similarities between them. Each object acts as a representation, as a medium through which one can create an identification around the unknown and the "stranger". What is read into this unknown itself transforms and these artefacts become elements in a process of cultural dialogue. Taken out of their dusty storerooms in the cellars of local and national museums they can now be made to enter a very different interactive context, one in which their very presence can address the public and recast the visitor's definition of past events.

(1) in Keith H. Basso *Portraits of the "Whiteman" - Linguistic play and cultural symbols among the Western Apache*, illustrations by Vincent Craig, published by Cambridge University Press 1979.
(2) I am grateful to Jonathan King for pointing out to me that the transformation of argillite from a soft to a hard substance is in itself a nineteeth century myth!
(3) see Meyer Fortes "Strangers" in *Studies in African Social Anthropology* ed. by M. Fortes & S. Patterson, Academic Press 1975.
(4) see Monica Wilson "Strangers in Africa: Reflections on Nyakyuusa, Nguni, and Sotho Evidence" in *Strangers in African Societies* ed. by William A. Shack & Elliot P. Skinner, University of California Press 1979.
(5) see Clementine Deliss *Exoticism and Eroticism: Representations of the Other in Early Twentieth Century French Anthropology* Ph.d thesis at School of Oriental and African Studies, University of London 1988.
(6) I include an excerpt of John Henrik Clarke's essay on "The reclaiming of African history" which refutes the idea of the absence of written histories in Africa.
"During the period in West African history - from the early part of the fourteenth century to the time of the Moroccan invasion in 1591, the city of Timbuctoo and the University of Sankore in the Songhay Empire was the intellectual center of Africa.... I will speak of one of the great black scholars of ancient Timbuctoo. Ahmed Baba was the last chancellor of the University of Sankore. He was one of the greatest African scholars of the late sixteenth century. His life is a brilliant example of the range and depth of West African intellectual activity before the colonial era. Ahmed Baba was the author of more than forty books, nearly every one of which had a different theme. He was in Timbuctoo when it was invaded by the Moroccans in 1591, and he was one of the first citizens to protest the occupation of his beloved home town. Ahmed Baba, along with other scholars, was imprisoned and eventually exiled to Morocco. During his expatriation from Timbuctoo, his collection of 1,600 books, one of the richest libraries of the day, was lost." In *African Culture: the Rhythms of Unity*, ed. by Molefi Kete Asante and Kariamu Welsh Asante, Africa World Press Inc. 1985.
(7) see p.8 in Cottie A. Burland *The Exotic White Man* published by Weidenfeld & Nicolson, London 1969.
(8) see Edward Graham Norris "Colon im Kontext - Versuch einer Deutung" *in Colon: das schwarze Bild vom weissen Mann* ed. by Jens Jahn, published by Rogner & Bernhard 1983.

Europeans on a tiger shoot
Cat. 81

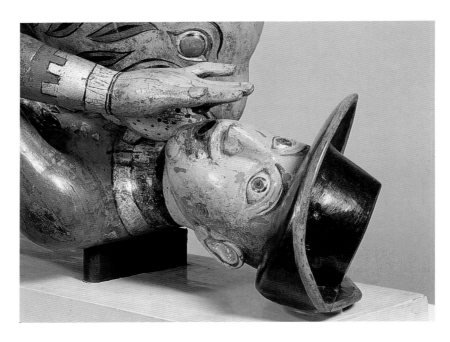

Tipu's Tiger
Cat. 80

A European lady with a dog
Cat. 77

Above: Four European figures with dog, games board,
and a bonsai
Cat. 67
Below: European Figure with bird and bonsai plant
Cat. 68

Western merchants inspecting silk samples
Cat. 76

above: Dance masks, Mexico
Cat. 103, 104
below: Dance masks, Guatemala
Cat. 88, 89, 90, 91

Appliquéd Fante flags
Cat. 4, 7

Pair of missionary angels, male and female
Cat. 28

Nigerian Images of Europeans: Commentary, Appropriation, Subversion.

JOHN PICTON

I was waiting for someone in an almost deserted market place in a village in Nigeria. At the time, in 1965, I was an employee of the Federal Government of Nigeria, in the Department of Antiquities; and I had been 'doing' fieldwork. Across the way, a group of boys were playing what was to them an obviously very funny game. One asked the others questions and pretended to write the answers in a notebook, moving a finger of one hand across the palm of the other. The solemnity of his performance was matched by the evident mirth of the others, for his questions and their answers were patently ridiculous, as only the questioner failed to notice. The joke was, of course, on me; and it was very funny.

Just as the British Islanders once suffered from one colonialism after another: Roman, Saxon, Norman . . . ; so too there is not a country in Africa that has not suffered at the expense of Europeans, whether via Mussolini and Marx in Ethiopia, or Mammon in Nigeria. Whatever one's reactions to all that, Africa and Europe are inevitably interrelated, historically and culturally, and always have been. To give one example, before the 'discovery' of the Americas, Africa was the source of all the gold in Europe; and we all know that the Portuguese exploration of the West African coast was initiated by the wish to subvert the control by Moroccan middlemen of access to gold, from West Africa, and pepper, from India. Transatlantic slavery and, later, colonialism were the result; and in the latter case, the wish to subvert the coastal middlemen was the immediate cause. The historical ironies in all of this will be manifest, some with consequences that were and, in many areas of the continent, continue to be horrific. Perhaps we are still too close to all of this to get a clear view; perhaps in a couple of hundred years . . . .

In the meantime, we must recognize that people are essentially pragmatic. Quite apart from the proposition that the changes in Africa over the last hundred years would probably have happened anyway, or something like them, no-one seriously advocates a return to a time when the present-day institutions and works of religion, learning, healthcare, communications, finance, and industrial technology were not there. Advocates of the Windsor Safari Park African Experience might think otherwise; but that view of Africa is morally and intellectually bogus. It assumes a spurious authenticity of an essentially European-invented traditionality that has very little to do with how real people lead real lives. This applies equally to the notions of tribe and ethnic group, both representing an imposition of identity from outside by means of which alien governments could rule their colonies and make them pay for it.

So, as white men and women came to be seen more and more often in towns and villages, what did people think of them? And are those thoughts embodied in art?

Europeans proved to be a paradoxical and ambivalent species. They had money, guns, patronage, power, authority; they provided education; and they were also capable of gross misunderstanding and ridicule; but they never had it all their own way. Their peculiarities were noted, and there was the ease with which one could provoke redfaced anger, and therein repay ridicule with ridicule; and they were easily manipulated. It is little wonder, then, that they appear within local traditions of visual culture.

Very often, the image of the European is motivated simply by an artistic curiosity about the presence of a European. On the other hand, the representation of a European may not be the representation of a European at all, but the appropriation of the image: the representation of Igbo deities as Europeans, on Owerri *mbari* houses (built as sacrifices to the gods in the face of impending disaster) would be a case in point. It would be absurd to suppose the European might be regarded as some kind of deity. Rather, the authority of the European provided an apt and immediately accessible image of the energy of a deity. Age-grade masks in the Edo-speaking part of Nigeria carved within the colonial period also incorporated images of Europeans, an image more recently displaced by the Nigerian soldier. These are among the images that are displayed at the celebrations of graduation from one grade to the next, and they are emblematic of the energy and strength of a group of young men who one day will emerge as elders. Here again, authority was visually redefined to fit present realities.

Clearly, one of the advantages of Europeans as subject matter in the works of art made by people in Africa is their wide-ranging utility, for example as figures of fun as well as icons of authority. Indeed, the appropriation of the European as a ready-made up-dated image of the authority of gods and of men could be said to work precisely because it was taken for granted that the authority represented in these images was not located in Europeans themselves. On the other hand,the representation of the authority of Europeans for what it is in itself seems always to have been a subject for a ridicule that was subversive of that authority. For example, there are the Europeans among the cast of comic characters in the *alarinjo* theatre of Yoruba people, sometimes including Queen Elizabeth and Prince Philip dancing together, as well as those creatures of the colonial presence, the policeman and the prostitute. On the doors carved by the famous sculptor, Areogun of Osi-Ilorin, we often find, standing on the mudguard of the district officer's bicycle, a thumb-sucking figure of the Yoruba trickster ready to subvert the pretence of the colonial order.

Finally, in any catalogue of Nigerian images of Europeans, we must include that devastating picture of colonial boredom, lethargy, and cynicism, by Demas Nwoko, *Nigeria in 1959*, the eve of Nigerian Independence; and we remember that fundamental irony of the colonial presence, that by introducing people to the political philosophies of Europe, which were in some sense presupposed in the colonial presence, the seeds of colonial demise and of Independence were also planted.

Demas Nwoko, *Nigeria in 1959*

The British Council as Cultural Catalyst in West Africa

CYPRIAN EKWENSI

The role played by the British Council in the development of modern African Literature can hardly be assessed. One must look back in some awe over the past decades between the early stirrings inspired by the British Council and the present blossom into the international scene. It would not be an exaggeration to say that the British Council could not have foreseen what a revolution it was starting in Africa, what fires it was setting alight, nor could it anticipate the unholy conflagration that would follow. Would it be right to claim that because of the diversionary effects of the rising new nationalism, little attention was paid to the work of the Council, or was it that one could not see the connection between cultural awareness and politics?

There was the Scribblers Club, in the late 1940s, born under the inspiration of Mr F. N. Lloyd Williams. At about that time the phenomenon known as Onitsha Market Literature was squealing in its infancy. My contribution to Onitsha Market Literature took the form of a novella called *WHEN LOVE WHISPERS*. Those chapbooks of 24 to 40 pages, paper-covered, were bought by traders at two shillings a copy, read and passed from hand to hand in Onitsha market till they were reduced to rags. Members of the Scribblers Club would meet in the evenings at the British Council, then housed on Custom Street near Tinubu Square in Lagos. The same street also housed the Glover Memorial Hall which served as a mass rallying point for political mobilisation against British Colonial rule. Radio Nigeria had a studio upstairs in the same hall. I used to broadcast my early short stories from there.

At the Tinubu Square end of the same Custom street the Public Relations Office under the tall, impressive and blonde-haired Harold Cooper battled with post World War II British propaganda, but kept its literary balance by publishing a magazine, *NIGERIA DIGEST,* in which I had two of my earliest stories published, *BIG MASSA* and *THE GORILLA OF UMO.* At the Scribblers Club meetings, literary efforts were tendered by members, read to the hearing of all present and mildly praised or ruthlessly damned in the manner of literary workshops. Every member listened keenly. No one had aspirations to winning the Nobel Prize for Literature, nor was there any motivation other than the exercise of our love for literature and the distant hope of one day breaking into print. That the colonial era was receiving its first serious demolition blows on the Gold Coast and in Nigeria from newly returned African *Argonauts* who had captured *The Golden Fleece* from America did not seem to bother the British Council. The Nigerianisation of the civil service and of commerce was yet a distant dream. The civil service and the government were securely in the hands of the British Administration, but the more experienced Administrators had learnt from the struggles in India that the wind of change was beginning to stir.

Today, Nigerian Literature is alive and dazzling, having distinguished itself internationally and in the Commonwealth. The Nigerian Cultural Policy was launched a few years back. Notable past events include the Black Arts Festival of 1964 and the colloquum of Festac 77.

Meanwhile, the British Council has developed from Cultural Catalyst to Technical Co-Operator, Project Implementer, but the initial role of interpreting British ways of life to Africa continues, adapting itself from the days of colonial rule into the turbulent period of self-rule and tenuous political climates. Through all this tinderbox existence the British Council has managed to thread warily and to survive.

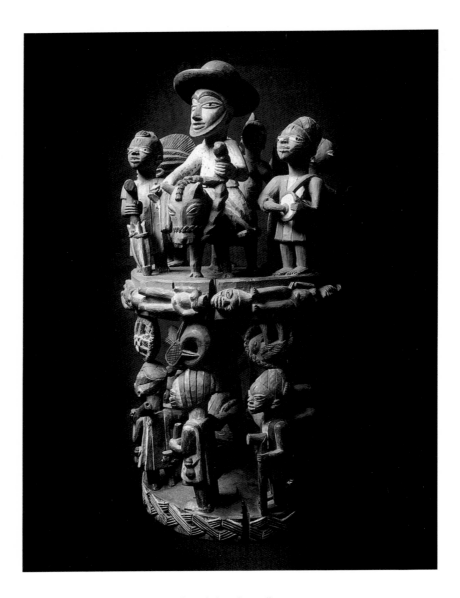

Abeokuta ensemble carving representing missionaries at dinner
Cat. 21
opposite: detail

European being carried in a litter supported by two natives
Cat. 19

Four European missionaries at dinner
Cat. 16

above: Figure of Queen Victoria Cat. 29
opposite: Bust of Queen Victoria Cat. 27

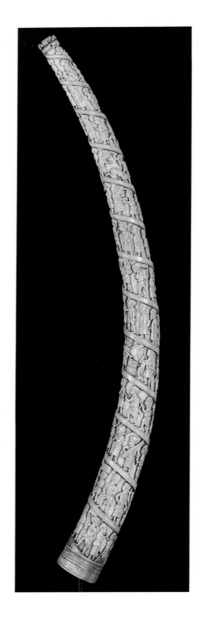

Carved ivory tusk Cat. 12
opposite: detail

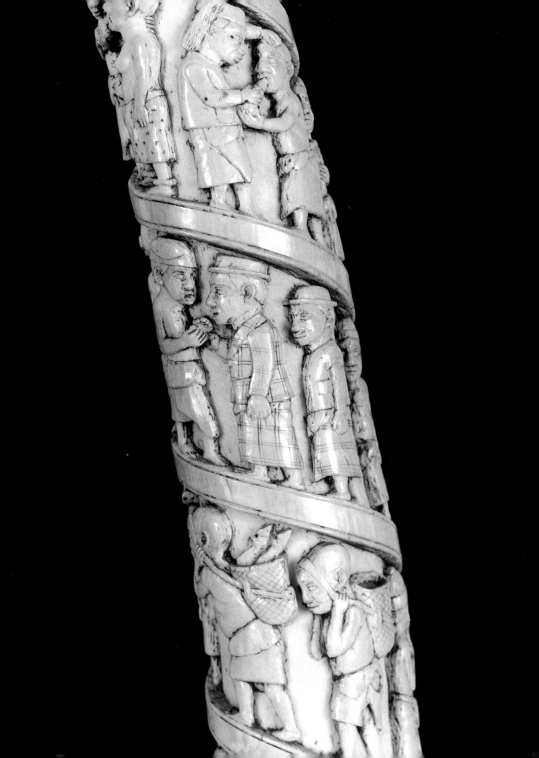

Carved ivory tusk representing a slave raid and the burning of a mission
Cat. 31

above: Figure of a European
Cat. 30
opposite: European corporal riding a horse
Cat. 20

above: Drum carved in the form of a European
Cat. 35
opposite: Male figures with removable hats
Cat: 37, 38, 39

Figures of Europeans
Cat. 51, 44, 50

Figure of a European
Cat. 47

Appliquéd Fante flag
Cat. 6

Appliquéd Fante flag
Cat. 3

above: Figure representing a European in German military uniform
Cat. 32
opposite: A white official with two policemen
Cat. 26

Armlet with African and Portuguese heads
Cat. 14

Model pistol
Cat. 11

above: Bust of Mary Kingsley
Cat. 17
left: Staff with European holding an umbrella
Cat. 33

Walking stick handle representing a missionary lady
Cat. 15
opposite: detail

Container, equestrian figure
Cat. 36
opposite: Ifa Divination Bowl
Cat. 25

physical size - no doubt an assessment of his charisma and social status - and attached floating to the shoulder of his woman. Obviously the man depends on the lady, perhaps not only emotionally, but also in his trading activities - if that was his profession. More interesting is the speculation that the woman may actually have been a Haida, since there were of course virtually no European women on the Northwest Coast at that time, and none in the Queen Charlotte Islands until the 1870s. Since in a matrilineal society inheritance passes through the female line, status is conferred on women whose children will inherit property from the mother's brothers - their uncles - rather than their father. So in this case the argillite figure ridiculing the man may have merely expressed a native view of property rights, and perhaps even suggested the man's acceptance of woman's position in Haida society. On the other hand the woman is not shown with a labret, or plug in the lower lip, the mark of a high ranking woman. So perhaps this woman was of low rank. Since prostitution in West Coast European cities such as Victoria was an early feature of Indian-white relations, the woman may actually not have been important in trade relations, but merely a sexual partner. If that is so then further explanation of the disparity in size is required. This may come, as suggested by Robin Wright [1], because prostitution, a wealth generating activity, was considered by the Haida a positive activity in a society in which wealth and status were interdependent .

Many other categories of Euro-American artefact were recreated in argillite, or occasionally in wood. European plates and very rarely cutlery were also carved in argillite. The plates were often of deeply carved circular platter form, the interiors carved with figurative designs of European advertising or American coins. The abstract designs included subjects probably derived from the shape of the paddle wheel of the *Beaver* - the first steamer in the Pacific - or the Japanese pie or chrysthanthemum design. At contact in the eighteenth century, Haida instruments included whistles, rattles and drums to assist at feasts and ceremonials. The Haida created recorders in stone to sell to pipe-playing sailors in the 1860s and 1870s. By that time however, the appalling effects of smallpox, European settlement, missionaries and technical disadvantages coincided with the first professional collecting of Haida artefacts. Collectors wanted used artefacts, and argillite carvers turned almost entirely to traditional Haida subject matter. During the long years of population decline in the first half of this century carving was kept alive by a few dedicated artists working in splendid isolation. The widespread revival of the 1970s, in which new sources of genius were tapped and celebrated, came again as a dialectic between white and native society, each acquiring new ideas and wealth. Today the souvenir shops of Washington, Alaska and British Columbia are choked with shoddy reproductions of argillite, often made in Asian factories. Clearly this is an abuse of cultural exclusivity. And yet at another level the Haida have created an ikon now implanted in the consciousness of the world. In the interpretation of argillite figures in European dress, or contemporary souvenir shop items, explanation must be derived from the context of the artefact both in Haida society, and within the relations of the Haida with the wider world.

(1) Much of the original scholarship on argillite derives from two Ph.d dissertations, *Changes in Haida Indian Argillite Carvings, 1820-1910* by C. Kaufmann, University of California, Los Angeles, 1969, and *Nineteenth Century Haida Argillite Pipe Carvers: Stylistic Attributions* by R. Wright, University of Washington, Seattle, 1985. Earlier interest was stimulated by Marius Barbeau, and Erna Gunther (who used the phrase Art made for Strangers), and taken up more recently by Bill Holm and Trisha Gessler.

above: Argillite panel pipe representing a steamboat with European figures and a dog
Cat. 55
below: Composite pipe bowl showing a European riding a horse, mounted on a paddle steamer
Cat. 57

Argillite carving of a European and his wife
Cat. 54

Netsuke, figure of a Dutchman
Cat. 61

Southern Barbarians or the Red-Haired People: The Japanese View of Exotic Europeans

TOSHIO WATANABE

A fierce storm diverted the course of a Chinese junk on the way to China from Siam in 1542/3. It reached Tanegashima, an island in southern Japan. There were three men of 'barbaric race from the South West' on board. In fact, they were Portuguese and this is the first recorded encounter between a Japanese and a European. There are some discrepancies between the various Western and Japanese records as to whether this happened in 1542 or 1543 and opinions vary as to whether muskets were introduced to Japan on this occasion or a year later. Nevertheless there is no doubt that the Japanese were fascinated by the Europeans and especially by the guns they brought. The local lord of Tanegashima bought two guns and tried to find out how to make them. Already within ten years guns were being manufactured in at least seven places in Japan .

For the next century or so, the Japanese showed deep curiosity and fascination with everything European from Christianity to playing cards. The appearance and mores of these strange Westerners became a favourite subject for contemporary Japanese painters and craftsmen. The Portuguese missionaries and tradesmen were depicted with glaring eyes and huge noses in genre paintings and in decorations on smart applied art objects. The Japanese called them the 'Southern Barbarians' and portray them as looking rather grotesque, a bit frightening, but above all exotic.

The name Southern Barbarians has its origin in China, where

anybody not from the Middle Kingdom, i.e. China, was regarded as some sort of barbarian. The Japanese knowledge of the world was at that time considerably more limited than the Chinese. Unlike China, Japan had no direct contact with Europe before the 16th century and the Japanese knew very little about Europe even by the mid-16th century, when the Portuguese arrived in Tanegashima. In fact before this event the term, Southern Barbarians, vaguely meant people from South East Asia. Even afterwards there was still quite a lot of confusion in Japan as to what Southern Barbarian culture actually was. Some studies indicate that the famous Tanegashima musket was not a European but a South East Asian type. The striped textiles, brought to Japan by the Portuguese and subsequently so popular among them, were also a South East Asian product. This is reminiscent of the 19th century Western confusion between Japanese and Chinese art, when many Chinese artefacts were regarded in the West as Japanese.

When the Europeans were finally expelled from Japan in 1639, only the Dutch were allowed to trade and keep a trading post on the man-made island of Deshima in Nagasaki . They were now called 'The Red-Haired People'. For the black-haired Japanese this was a clear enough definition of a people belonging to the other culture. They were still depicted with big eyes and huge noses, but now often additionally with red hair. The tradition of grotesque-looking Westerners continues even after active contact was renewed from the mid-19th century onwards. The West became very fashionable again in Japan.

The most characteristic manifestation of this can be seen in the so-called *Yokohama-e* (Yokohama pictures) prints. These were enormously popular and there are over 800 prints known. They are mostly genre pictures, depicting life in the city of Yokohama. A large number of them depict Westerners and their way of life with an emphasis on their otherness. Strange habits and costumes are lovingly shown, often using stylistic techniques, such as shading and perspective, which were thought to be Western. Most of this type of *Yokohama-e* were published within a fairly short period during the 1860s. Foreigners from the five major Western nations (America, Britain, France, Prussia and Russia) appear frequently and are specified as such in the captions. However they are mostly interchangeable and the Japanese artists do not differentiate very much between the nations. From the Japanese point of view, they were all strange but fascinating exotic foreigners.

Japan has a habit of nurturing its own culture by adapting elements of foreign culture. Both during the 16th and the 19th centuries it was not China but the West which caught the imagination of the Japanese. During these two key periods of intense contact with the West, images of Europeans became major genre subjects showing the voracious curiosity of the Japanese about those people whom they perceived to be exotic.

An Englishman and a Chinese from Nanking
Cat. 63

A European with a courtesan
Cat. 62

The Chinese View

CRAIG CLUNAS

Chinese culture possessed a fully formed literary and visual stereotype of 'the other' many centuries before Portuguese ships first sailed into East Asian waters in 1514. The principal carrier of this was Buddhism, formed in India and transmitted to China after about AD 100. Buddhism's roots in the regions to the west of China, regions from which it was separated by relatively impenetrable mountains and deserts, meant that for early China the 'Far West' was the source of the inscrutable, generally tinged with elements of a higher spiritual power. Up to about 1500, the visual components of the stereotype related almost entirely to men, and reflected a simple reversal of Chinese expectations about masculine beauty.

Prominent noses, curly hair, and heavily bearded chins are the distinguishing marks of the figures of exotic grooms who hold their master's horses in the aristocratic tombs of the Tang dynasty (618-906).Chinese craft producers similarly had a long history of filling specific needs in the export market to other Asian states. They were therefore capable immediately of manufacturing a wide range of products to suit the new demands of European customers. These ranged from ceramics decorated in underglaze blue with the coats of arms of Portuguese adventurers, to lacquered furniture imitating the more sought after Japanese pieces. By the late seventeenth century, a major trade had developed in craft goods, which supplemented the more lucrative trade in tea, raw silk, drugs and precious metals. These Chinese export artefacts are often decorated with subjects supplied by the Western merchants who purchased them, and often exhibit a degree of tension between the western conventions of representation, and the Chinese stereotypes of foreign peoples. The 'Western ocean' people were assimilated with ease to the old large-nosed, curly-haired tradition, which was to endure until the shock of imperialism after the 1840s led to the formation of a new image of the aggressor.

Jesuit missionaries active in China around 1600 made the next major contribution to the formation of the stereotype. Aware (quite correctly) that the imagery of the Crucifixion would be simply repellent to Chinese sensibilities, and anxious to distance themselves from the heretic Dutch and English merchants, they concentrated on the icon of the Madonna and Child as the focus of worship. By the end of the Ming dynasty (1368-1644) most educated Chinese knew that the Westerner's God was a woman holding a baby, depicted in art works which seemed startlingly three-dimensional. This remained a quintessential visual image of the West in later Chinese art, not least in the vogue at the imperial court in the eighteenth century for a sort of 'Europeanisme', a parallel to the fashion for 'Chinoiserie' in contemporary Europe. The image of the Madonna was by Chinese standards exceedingly immodest, and supported the stereotype of the sexually available Western woman. Thus sensual freedom and soulless technical ingenuity gradually replaced esoteric wisdom as the defining characteristics of the Western 'other'.

In general, however, there was little interest in 16th-19th century China in portraying foreigners at all, and the bulk of the objects with foreign subjects on them were made for the export market. The punch bowl with images of the radical politician John Wilkes (Cat. 73), and the mug showing a hunt in full cry (Cat. 74) would have been manufactured in conditions where only their painters and the merchants involved would have encountered them. There is an effort by the porcelain enamellers to
copy as precisely as possible their printed model. It is a measure of their success that there is no hint in Western sources that these ceramics were viewed as exotic. Rather they were valued as durable and attractive imports which existed comfortably within the existing visual culture. This sort of imagery scarcely entered the consciousness of Chinese society at all.

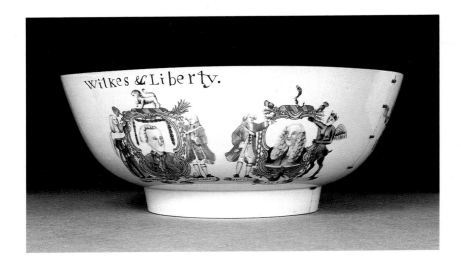

above: Punch bowl
Cat. 73
opposite: Mug
Cat. 74

A European lady in Indian dress

Europeans in Indian Art

J.P. LOSTY

Foreigners *per se* were of little interest in the classical periods of Indian sculpture and painting up to AD 1200, concerned as they were with the making immanent of the divine through the prescribed rules of iconography. Indian art has in any case always been more concerned with types than with individuals, so that any foreign type immediately recognisable as exotic could be used traditionally to represent a particular foreigner. With the exception of two brief periods, during the climax of Mughal painting from 1590-1630, and in the first half of the l9th century, this remained true for Indian contact with Europeans also.

Apart from contact in classical times and adventurers like Marco Polo, Europeans first reached India via the long voyage round Africa in 1498. The Portuguese, and the Dutch and English after them, were initially in search of trade in spices, which were to be found more in Indonesia than India itself. Indian textiles, however, were at this time the best produced and cheapest in the world, so that it was not long before they were flooding into Europe, and in styles and patterns designed for the European market. Quilted bed coverlets in particular were embroidered with figures in Portuguese dress, in a riot of assorted classical and Indian motifs. These however were made solely for export, and it is not until the late 16th century that we find any serious interest in representing foreigners in paintings meant for the cultivated taste of Indian patrons themselves.

Serious Indian artistic response to a foreign presence can be assessed on two levels. Foreigners brought as gifts European paintings and prints which were highly prized by the Mughals. In particular they required their artists to learn from them the European techniques of modelling, foreshortening, perspective, etc., all of which were used to add realism to Mughal painting. There are many Mughal paintings of the late 16th and early 17th centuries which are direct copies of European works, or caprices based on elements of several, which show how artists experimented with these techniques, which they then incorporated into Mughal paintings with traditional literary or historical content. All this made possible a true art of portraiture, instead of figures based on stylised literary types. The portraits of important figures at court were carefully recorded and labelled in the studio, so that in paintings illustrating recent history or scenes at the contemporary court, their exact appearance at the right age could be included. In this way Europeans such as the Jesuits who paid several visits to Akbar's court in the late 16th century were incorporated into Mughal historical paintings. Such foreigners were stylistically represented in the normal Mughal way, although dressed in contemporary European clothes.

Mughal painting is eclectic, and uses Indian, Persian or European elements indifferently in order to express its aims. Jahangir (1605-27) thought of himself as the apex of the cultured world, and in some of the paintings most closely associated with his idea of his own kingship, foreign rulers are incorporated to serve politico-cultural aims. Thus contemporary rulers such as the Ottoman Sultan or King James I of England were relegated to the outer parts of the painting, while Jahangir and his immediate male family and entourage occupy the centre. The image of King James was brought by Sir Thomas Roe, the English ambassador to Jahangir, and it and other Tudor and Stuart portrait miniatures and European portrait medallions and cameos after the antique, had considerable influence on the iconography of Mughal royal portraiture. Such paintings are but the most extreme examples illustrating the prime purpose of Mughal, or indeed of Indian painting in general, which is the expression of the royal patron's power and prestige. Europeans in court or durbar paintings, in subordinate positions as foreign ambassadors, enhanced the prestige of the royal central figure.

In later, more hedonistic Mughal paintings, European men and women are to be found often dressed in the styles of the 16th century, standing on carpets of flowers. In this they are no different from similar paintings of beautiful youths and maidens of the Mughal court. Later, other elements creep in. European female dress acquired subtly erotic elements, and ladies who wear it, whether Indian or European is not always clear, eye the viewer with a frankly come-hither air. The point is emphasised by their often holding bottles and wine cups, and by the addition of dogs. Neither Hindu nor Muslim culture had much time for dogs as pets, and the fondness of Europeans for these animals exposed them to the charge of uncleanliness from Indians. We would not be wrong, also to see an element of mockery in such paintings, a trend which intensified in the British period.

As Europeans began to acquire political power in India, some had themselves painted by Mughal artists in a manner emphasising their power and prestige, precisely as such paintings had been used in the high Mughal period. The "Company" schools generally favoured by European patrons in this period rarely included portraits of Europeans, as the subjects selected were invariably meant to be mementos of India. An exception is found at those courts which had succumbed almost totally to European influence, such as the late Mughal courts at Murshidabad and Lucknow, and here important visitors such as the British Resident or the Governor-General were shown in formal durbar scenes. Such scenes are also found in paintings from those courts where European influence was still minimal, such as the courts of Rajasthan, or else ignored, as in the Mughal court painting at Delhi during the first half of the 19th century. Regardless of the technique used, these images convey the traditional purpose of court paintings, the exaltation of the king above his court.

The Mughal Emperor had been in the East India Company's power since 1803, but in durbar paintings he is still shown sitting enthroned high above the ranks of the nobility, among whom stands respectfully the British Resident, clad in the blue uniform of the political service. It is instructive to compare two versions of the visit to Udaipur in 1855 of Sir Henry Lawrence, the Governor-General's Agent for Rajputana, and his staff. In one, an oil painting by F.C. Lewis, who was present in Udaipur at the meeting, the British sit on low stools or cushions, relatively relaxed and comfortable, while the court is fairly informal. Although Lewis follows Indian tradition in placing the Maharana Sarup Singh at the centre of the picture, he is not exalted above all the court as he is in the Udaipur court artist Tara's version of the scene, with the four British officers clad in blue uniforms kneeling stiffly before him along with the other members of the court. Exotic and powerful the foreigners may be, but the Indian artist well knew how to use them to enhance his master's prestige.

An official of the Indian Political Service in uniform, accompanied by two ladies and two small girls, the latter in tweed coats
Cat. 85

شپ کرنیل ہاکو بصاحب

An elderly man, Colonel Jacob Petrus, smoking a hookah
Cat. 83

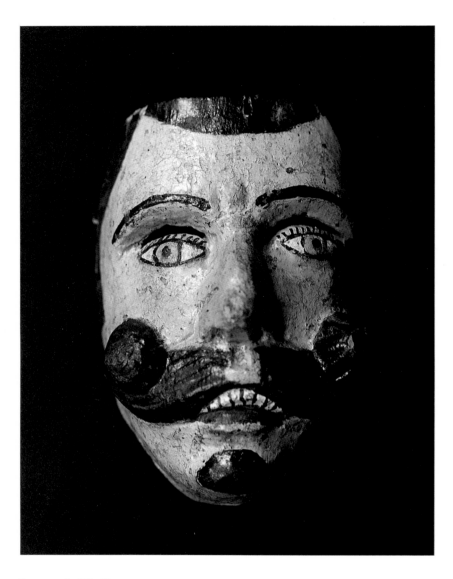

Dance mask of the Marquez
Cat. 102

Masks in Latin America: Old World Identities on New World Faces

CHLOË SAYER

It is nearly 500 years since Columbus first sailed into American waters. Exploitation soon followed exploration. By 1521 Hernán Cortés had secured the Conquest of Mexico for Spain; in 1532 Francisco Pizarro defeated the Incas of Peru with a fighting force of 180 men and 27 horses. Although events are usually described from a Spanish perspective, the inhabitants of the New World left their own accounts, with descriptions of the *conquistadores*. In Mexico a messenger from the Gulf Coast warned Moctezuma, the Aztec emperor, about the arrival of 'strange people' travelling in 'towers or small mountains floating on the waves of the sea... They have very light skin, much lighter than ours. They all have long beards, and their hair comes only to their ears'. The people of Peru were also surprised by the physical appearance of the invaders, who dressed in a peculiar way and 'went about on enormous animals with silver feet'.

Colonisation, Independence and twentieth-century modernisation have affected the Indian peoples of Latin America to widely varying degrees. Many retain a strong cultural identity. Quechua, the language of the Inca empire, is still spoken by millions of Sierra Indians. In Mexico and Guatemala approximately 70 languages remain. Despite the spread of Christianity and the adoption of many European customs, most indigenous peoples maintain craft skills, beliefs and ceremonies which link them with their ancestors.

In rural areas, where life is often extremely hard, festivals mark the high point of village life. Usually they commemorate Catholic holidays and honour the local patron saint. Dances, of pre-Conquest and European origin, are an important element and vary according to region. In some towns *mestizos* (Mexicans of mixed European and Indian descent) also perform masked dances. To an outsider celebrations might suggest mere spectacle, but the purpose is deeply serious. Dancers are motivated by religious devotion: they know they are ensuring the well-being of their families, and promoting divine harmony for the community at large.

Although costumes and masks are sometimes costly, performers bear the financial burden gladly. Masks transform and elevate the wearer; they superimpose a new face. In pre-Hispanic times masks enabled shamans to mediate between the interdependent worlds of gods, animals, plants and men; today they still inspire a sense of awe. Often masks are made from wood by skilled craftsmen, who also earn a living carving Christian saints. Alternative materials include gourds, leather, paper, cloth, wire mesh and wax.

Europeans, with their fair skins, facial hair and blue or green eyes, are a great source of inspiration. So, too, are the heavily-bearded *Moros* (Moors), who occupied Spain for almost 800 years, and who are trad-itionally regarded as villains. Numerous Mexican dances belong to the cycle of 'Moors and Christians'; they show masked Spanish soldiers defending their homeland against invasion and ultimately defeating their foes. Some dances involve only Moors. During *Carnaval* in the State of Morelos performers known as *Chinelos* wear wire-mesh masks with black horse-hair beards, velvet robes and tall hats replete with fringing, beads and, increasingly, battery-powered light bulbs. History is also kept alive by dances portraying the Conquest of Mexico and Guatemala. In countless villages performers do battle as Spaniards and Indians; in the end the vanquished accept the Catholic faith, and renounce their treasures.

The most important role in many such dances is that of *Santiago Caballero* (Saint James). Brandishing a cross and riding a white horse, he leads his followers to victory. The horse, carved from wood in one or two sections, is tied round the waist. Náhuatl-speaking villagers in San Miguel Tzinacapan, Puebla, regard the horse with especial veneration. At the end of each fiesta, *Santiago Caballero* entrusts it to his successor, who promises to keep it near the house altar and to provide it with fresh water and maize.

The European physiognomy dominates a great range of dances. During *Carnaval* in the State of Mexico dancers wear handsome wax masks; the hair from cows' tails is used for eyebrows and beards, which may be dyed bright colours for comic effect. Spectacle frames are also popular. Performers impersonate fine 'gentlemen'; when performing elegant quadrilles, they are partnered by male villagers showily dressed as women. An element of parody is also present in the *Chonguinada*. This dance, performed near Huancayo in Peru, requires male dancers to take the role of *Españoles* and *Españolas*. Masks are made from painted wire mesh, and decorated with real hair.

Under Spanish rule plays were an important instrument of evangelisation. Today Catholic saints and friars still appear in masked dance-dramas deriving from the miracle plays of ancient Spain; European in appearance, their features are often highly idealised. In some regions, however, *ermitaños* (hermit priests) serve as buffoons. This lack of reverence caused the editor of *Alegre*, a nineteenth-century journal, to criticise government authorities for allowing carnival maskers to dress as 'popes, bishops, cardinals and friars, making monkeys of themselves to mock most indecently the dignitaries of the Church...'.

African settlers, brought to Mexico as slaves after the Spanish Conquest, also appear in several dances. Performers disguised as *Negros* (blackmen) sometimes act as clowns, telling ribald jokes and keeping the crowd in order. In the State of Michoacán, however, *Negros* are thought by the Purépecha Indians to represent lordly beings who control the air. Their masks are finely carved and their attire is often spectacular.

Masks in Latin America are made to be worn. They can be admired out of context, but only through dance can their wit, grace, splendour or terror be fully communicated.

above: Mask representing a French soldier
Cat. 95
opposite: Tejorón mask
Cat. 99

Catalogue

Italicised names before place-names signify indigenous groups

Asterix denotes illustration

1

Asante Gold Weights
representing:
equestrian figure L. 5.4 cms
seated figure H. 6.2 cms
coffin L. 7.4 cms
lock and key H. 3.2 cms
rifle L. 6.4 cms
four-cannoned gun H. 5 cms
cannon L. 8.3 cms
cannon L. 3.1 cms
cannon L. 4 cms
cartridge belt L. 5.5 cms
key H. 3.2 cms
brass, and other metal inlay
Asante, Ghana
Lent by the Board of Trustees of the National Museums and Galleries on Merseyside, Liverpool Museum

2

Umbrella finial in the form of a gun
Asante, Ghana
circa 19th century
L. 34.2 cms
Lent by the Trustees of The British Museum, Ethnography Department, London

3*

Appliquéd Fante flag, with whale and boats motif
Proverb: "I am the great whale which capsizes sailing ships, I am master of all creatures of the sea."
cotton fabric, patchwork appliqué
Fante, Asafo, Ghana
circa early-mid 20th century
H. 111 cms L. 147 cms
Lent by Peter Adler, London

4*

Appliquéd Fante flag with bridge motif
Proverb: "No enemy can cross the bridge that leads to our village."
cotton fabric, patchwork appliqué
Fante, Asafo, Ghana
circa early-mid 20th century
H. 87 cms L. 149 cms
Lent by Peter Adler, London

5

Appliquéd Fante flag, with train motif
Proverb: "Our Company like the great Kumasi train is powerful and always ready to go."
cotton fabric, patchwork appliqué
Fante, Asafo, Ghana
circa early-mid 20th century
H. 96 cms L. 124 cms
Lent by Peter Adler, London

6*
Appliquéd Fante flag, with heraldic motif
cotton fabric, patchwork appliqué
Fante, Asafo, Ghana
circa early-mid 20th century
H. 96 cms L. 156 cms
Lent by Peter Adler, London

7*
Appliquéd Fante flag, with aeroplane motif
Proverb: "I the Chief have an aeroplane which flies in the sky. If you take delight in it I can allow you to see all that is in it."
cotton fabric, patchwork appliqué
Fante, Asafo, Ghana
circa early-mid 20th century
H. 92 cms L. 153 cms
Lent by Peter Adler, London

8
Appliquéd Fante flag, with heraldic motif
Proverb: 'We are the two great beasts that guard the crown so that our leader cannot be overthrown."
cotton fabric, patchwork appliqué
Fante, Asafo, Ghana
circa early-mid 20th Century
H. 97 cms L. 162 cms
Lent by Peter Adler, London

9
Appliquéd Fante flag, with bird and castle motif
Proverb: "No enemy can take us by surprise and open the lock to our fort - for the cock will crow a warning and our soldiers and wild beasts will defend us."
cotton fabric, patchwork appliqué
Fante, Asafo, Ghana
circa early-mid 20th centurry
H. 82 cms L. 162 cms
Lent by Peter Adler, London

10
Tobacco pipe bowl
ceramic, paint
Ghana (Gold Coast)
circa late 19th century
L. 8.1 cms
Lent by the Trustees of The British Museum, Ethnography Department, London

11*
Model pistol
wood
Ghana
circa 19th century
L. 28.5 cms
Lent by Michael Graham-Stewart, London

12*
Carved ivory tusk
Loango, West Africa
H. 105 cms
Lent by Peter Adler, London

13
Carved ivory tusk
Loango, West Africa
H. 105 cms
Lent by Peter Adler, London

14*
**Armlet with African and
Portuguese heads**
metal (bronze)
Bini, Benin, Nigeria
circa 18th century
L. 14.6 cms
Lent by the Board of Trustees of the
National Museum and Galleries on
Merseyside, Liverpool Museum

15*
**Walking stick handle representing
a missionary lady**
(Figure possibly that of Mary
Slessor, a missionary in Old Calabar)
wood
Calabar, Eastern Nigeria
circa 1890s - early 1900s
H. 89 cms
Lent by Ipswich Museums, Ipswich
Borough Council

16*
**Four European missionaries at
dinner**
Artist: Thomas Ona Odulate of
Ijebu-Ode
wood
Lagos, Nigeria
circa mid 20th century
H. 22 cms
Lent by the Archaeology Section,
City of Bristol Museum and Art
Gallery

17*
Bust of Mary Kingsley
wood, pigment
Qua-Ibo, Nigeria
circa late 19th - early 20th century
H. 40 cms W. 22 cms
Lent by the Board of Trustees of the
National Museum and Galleries on
Merseyside, Liverpool Museum

18
Gelede mask of a European
painted wood
Yoruba, Nigeria
circa late 19th - early 20th century
L. 33 cms
Lent by the Trustees of The British
Museum, Ethnography Department,
London

19*
**European being carried in a litter
supported by two natives**
wood
Yoruba, Nigeria
circa early 20th century
L. 15.2 cms H. 12.8 cms
Lent by Manchester Museum,
University of Manchester

20*
European corporal riding a horse
painted wood
Yoruba, Nigeria
circa 1890
H. 36.5 cms
Lent by Michael Graham-Stewart,
London

21*
Abeokuta ensemble carving
representing missionaries at dinner
painted wood
Yoruba, Nigeria
circa late 19th century
H. 82.5 cms
Lent by Royal Pavilion Art Gallery
and Museums, Brighton

22
Figure of Queen Victoria
blackened wood
Yoruba, Nigeria
circa late 19th - early 20th century
H. 36.5 cms W. 13.5 L. 15.5 cms
Lent by the Board of Trustees of the
National Museum and Galleries on
Merseyside, Liverpool Museum

23
Figure of a European
Artist: Bamgboye of Odo Owa
wood
Yoruba, Odo-Owa, Illqrin
Province, Northern Nigeria
circa early - mid 20th century
H. 30.5 cms
Lent by the Trustees of The British
Museum, Ethnography Department,
London

24
Gelede mask
'The Brazilian'
painted wood
Yoruba, Southwestern Nigeria
circa mid - late 19th century
L. 17.6 cms
Lent by the Trustees of The British
Museum, Ethnography Department,
London

25*
Ifa Divination Bowl
painted wood
Western Yoruba Ifa, Ile-Ife (Ketu
area), Southwestern Nigeria
H. 38 cms D. 32 cms
Lent by Ipswich Museums, Ipswich
Borough Council

26*
A white official with two
policemen
painted wood
Western Yoruba, Southern Nigeria
circa early 20th century
H. 64 cms W. 48 cms
Lent by the Trustees of The British
Museum, Ethnography Department,
London

27*
Figure of Queen Victoria
cottonwood
Yoruba, Southern Nigeria
circa late 19th - early 20th century
H. 40.6 cms
Lent by the Trustees of The British
Museum, Ethnography Department,
London

28*
Pair of missionary angels, male
and female
cottonwood
Southern Nigeria
circa early 20th century
each H. 42 cms D. 8.6 cms
Lent by Manchester Museum,
University of Manchester

29*
Bust of Queen Victoria
painted wood
Mende, Sierra Leone
circa late 19th century
H. 34.5 cms W. 14 cms D. 16 cms
Lent by The Horniman Museum and
Public Park Trust

30*
Figure of a European, standing
painted wood
possibly *Kamba*, Kenya
circa 19th century
H. 25.5 cms
Lent by Michael Graham-Stewart,
London

31*
Carved ivory tusk representing a
slave raid and the burning of a
mission
ivory
Loango, West Africa
circa 19th century
H. 50.8 cms
Lent by the Trustees of The British
Museum, Ethnography Department,
London

32*
Figure representing a European in
German military uniform
(Probably Wilhelm II)
painted wood
Toga, West Africa
circa late 19th century
H. 118 cms W. 29.5 cms D. 18 cms
Lent by The Horniman Museum and
Public Park Trust

33*
Staff with European holding an
umbrella
wood
Congo
circa 1900
H. 86 cms
Lent by Michael Graham-Stewart,
London

34
European being carried in a litter
supported by two natives
ivory
Loanda, W. Congo
circa 1900
L. 24 cms W. 4 cms
Lent by Manchester Museum,
University of Manchester

35
Drum carved in the form of a
European
wood, paint, glass, serpent skin
Bakongo, Zaire
circa late 19th century
H. 113 cms W. 28.5 cms
Lent by the Trustees of The British
Museum, Ethnography Department,
London

36*
Container, equestrian figure
Artist: Voania Muba of Bowoyo
village
ceramic
Bakongo, Zaire, Lower Congo
circa early 20th century
H. 50 cms
Lent by the Trustees of The British
Museum, Ethnography Department,
London

37*
Male figure with removable hat
painted wood
Tanzania
circa 1920s
H. 44.5 cms W. 18 cms
Lent by Royal Pavilion Art Gallery
and Museums, Brighton

38*
Male figure with removable hat
painted wood
Tanzania
circa 1920s
H. 35.5 cms W. 10 cms
Lent by Royal Pavilion Art Gallery
and Museums, Brighton

39*
Male figure with removable hat
painted wood
Tanzania
circa 1920s
H. 35.5 cms W. 11 cms
Lent by Royal Pavilion Art Gallery
and Museums, Brighton

40
Seated European reading a book
painted wood
Chokwee or *Lunda*, Angola
circa early 20th century
H. 17 cms
Lent by Michael Graham-Stewart,
London

41
Stool with European figure support
wood
Rotse or *Lozi*, Zambia
circa 1900
H. 45 cms
Lent by Michael Graham-Stewart,
London

42
Model rifle
wood
Zimbabwe or Malawi
circa 20th century
L. 97 cms
Lent by Michael Graham-Stewart,
London

43
Model pistol
wood, metal
Shona, Zimbabwe
circa 19th century
L. 36 cms
Lent by Michael Graham-Stewart,
London

44*
Figure of a white woman
painted wood
Rhodesia
circa late 19th - early 20th century
H. 35.5 cms
Lent by Calderdale Museums & Arts

45
Calabash, engraved with a ship and anchor
gourd, pigment
Sierra Leone
circa 19th century
H. 53 cms W. 23 cms
Lent by the Board of Trustees of the National Museum and Galleries on Merseyside, Liverpool Museum

46
Staff with Portuguese official
wood
Mozambique
circa 1900
H. 97.5 cms
Lent by Michael Graham-Stewart, London

47*
Figure of a European
painted wood
Sotho, Transvaal
circa 1900
H. 37 cms
Lent by Ipswich Museums, Ipswich Borough Council

48*
Figure of a European wearing a cap and blazer
painted wood
Sotho, Transvaal
circa 1900
H. 28 cms
Lent by Ipswich Museums, Ipswich Borough Council

49
Spoon carved in the shape of a man
painted wood
Sotho, Transvaal
circa 1900
H.29 cms
Lent by Ipswich Museums, Ipswich Borough Council

50*
Figure of a white man standing
painted wood
South Africa
circa 19th - early 20th century
H. 19 cms
Lent by Calderdale Museums & Arts

51*
Figure of a European and chair
painted wood
South Africa
circa 19th - early 20th century
H. 21 cms
Lent by Calderdale Museums & Arts

52
Comb surmounted by a figure wearing a hat and smoking a pipe
wood
Northwest Coast, North America
circa before 1870
H. 17.1 cms
Lent by the Trustees of The British Museum, Ethnography Departmen London

53
Argillite panel pipe with designs
borrowed from British trade goods
Haida, Queen Charlotte Islands,
British Columbia, Canada
circa 1830s
L. 35.5 cms
Lent by the Trustees of The British
Museum, Ethnography Department,
London

54*
Argillite carving of a European and
his wife
Haida, Queen Charlotte Islands,
British Columbia, Canada
circa 1840s
H. 23.1 cms
Lent by the Trustees of The British
Museum, Ethnography Department,
London

55*
Argillite panel pipe representing a
steamboat with European figures
and a dog
argillite, bone
Haida, Queen Charlotte Islands,
British Columbia, Canada
circa 1840s
H. 10.5 cms L. 34.5 cms
Lent by the Trustees of The British
Museum, Ethnography Department,
London

56
Argillite "deckhouse" panel pipe
argillite, ivory or bone
Haida, Queen Charlotte Islands,
British Columbia, Canada
circa 1840s
L. 21.3 cms H. 7.2 cms
Lent by the Archaeology Section,
City of Bristol Museum and Art
Gallery

57*
Composite pipe bowl showing a
European riding a horse, mounted
on a paddle steamer
wood, bone, pigment
Haida, Queen Charlotte Islands,
British Columbia, Canada
circa 1840s
L. 30.5 ans
Lent by Ipswich Museums, Ipswich
Borough Council

58
Argillite panel pipe with "block-
and-tackle" motif
Haida, Queen Charlotte Islands,
British Columbia, Canada
circa 1840s
L. 37 cms H. 5 cms W. 2.8 cms
Lent by the Board of Trustees of the
National Museum and Galleries on
Merseyside, Liverpool Museum

59
Argillite panel pipe with three European figures and a dog
Haida, Queen Charlottee Islands, British Columbia, Canada
circa 1840s
L. 28 cms H. 7.8 cms W. 2.3 cms
Lent by the Board of Trustees of the National Museum and Galleries on Merseyside, Liverpool Museum

60
Ivory carving with incised image of sailing ship
walrus ivory
Alaska, United States
L. 3.8 cms
Lent by the Board of Trustees of the National Museum and Galleries on Merseyside, Liverpool Museum

61*
Netsuke, figure of a Dutchman
wood
Japan
circa 18th century
H. 11.7 cms
Lent by Eskenazi Limited, London

62*
A European with a courtesan
Artist: Eisho
watercolour print on paper
Japan
circa 1800
H. 25A cms W. 38.1 cms
Lent by the Victoria & Albert Museum

63*
An Englishman and a Chinese from Nanking
Artist: Sadahide
watercolour print on paper
Japan
circa 1861
H. 34.6 cms W. 24.1 cms
Lent by the Victoria & Albert Museum

64
The Americans
Artist: Ikket
watercolour print on paper
Japan
circa 1872
H. 24.5 cms W. 16.5 cms
Lent by Sir Hugh Cortazzi

65
Two foreigners frightening Japanese people
Unsigned
watercolour print on paper
Japan
circa 1890
H. 35 cms W. 22 cms
Lent by Sir Hugh Cortazzi

66
Figure group, a European couple
porcelain, made at Dehua in Fujian province, with enamels and gilding added in the Netherlands
China
circa 1690 - 1730
H. 16.S cms
Lent by the Victoria & Albert Museum

67*
Four European figures, man and
woman, boy and girl, with dog,
games board, and a bonsai
blanc de chine
China
circa 18th century
H. 15 cms W. 16.5 cms D. 6.5 cms
Lent by Durham University, Oriental
Museum

68*
European Figure with bird and
bonsai plant
blanc de chine
China
circa 18th century
H. 7.5 cms W. 5 cms D. 5.4 cms
Lent by Durham University, Oriental
Museum

69
Snuff bottle with European figures
enamel
China
circa mid-late 18th century
H. 5.8 cms W. 3.5 cms D. 2 cms
Lent by Durham University, Oriental
Museum

70
Enamelled bowl with European
figures in a Chinese landscape
enamel
China
circa mid-late 18th century
H. 3.8 cms D. 11.6 cms
Lent by Durham University, Oriental
Museum

71
Plate, decorated with a European
family in a landscape
painted enamels on copper
China
circa 1730-1745
D. 35.2 cms
Lent by the Victoria & Albert
Museum

72
Flask, decorated with European
figures
porcelain painted in enamels
China
mark of the Qianlong reign (1736-
1795), circa 1740-1760
H. 17.2cms
Lent by the Victoria & Albert
Museum

73*
Punch bowl, decorated with the
slogan 'Wilkes and Liberty'
porcelain painted in enamels
China
circa 1770-1775
D. 26 cms
Lent by the Victoria & Albert
Museum

74*
Mug, decorated with a hunting
scene
porcelain painted in underglaze blue
and enamels
China
circa 1770-1785
H. 20.3 cms
Lent by the Victoria & Albert

Museum

75
Tea packing warehouse
watercolour on paper
Canton, China
circa 1800
H. 54 cms W. 39.6 cms
Lent by the Victoria & Albert
Museum

76*
Western merchants inspecting silk
samples
watercolour on silk
Canton, China
circa 1880-1900
Lent by the Victoria & Albert
Museum

77*
A European lady with a dog
watercolour with gold on paper
India
circa 1640
H. 13.9 cms W. 8.6 cms
Lent by the India Office Library
(British Library)

78
A European youth
watercolour
India
circa 1680
H. 139 cms W. 8.6 cms
Lent by the India Office Library
(British Library)

79*
A European lady in Indian dress
watercolour with gold on paper
India
circa 1700
H. 19.8 cms W. 11.2 cms
Lent by the India Office Library
(British Library)

80*
Replica of 'Tipu's Tiger'
The original mechanical organ, now
in the Victoria & Albert Museum,
was made for the Tipu Sultan, the
Indian ruler of Mysore (1750-1799).
It represents a tiger devouring a
British soldier.
fibreglass, paint
L. 190 cms H. 84 cms W. 50 cms
Lent by the Trustees of the National
Museums of Scotland

81*
Europeans on a tiger shoot
Company School,
watercolour
Patiala, Punjab, India
circa 1892
Lent by the Victoria & Albert
Museum

82
**European hunter with fowling
piece and dog**
gouache with gold on paper
Rajasthan, Devgarh, India
circa 1810-20
H. 19 W. 28 cms
Private Collection

83*
An elderly man, Colonel Jacob
Petrus, smoking a hookah
gouache on paper
Delhi, India
circa 1840
H. 22.1 cms W. 16.8 cms
Lent by the India Office Library
(British Library)

84
English child with her South
Indian Ayah
Company School,
watercolour
South India
circa 1840
H. 24.1 cms W. 19 cms
Private Collection

85*
An official of the Indian Political
Service in uniform, accompanied
by two ladies and two small girls,
the latter in tweed coats
gouache on paper
Kotah, India
circa 1870
H. 16 cms W. 13.1 cms
Lent by the India Office Library
(British Library)

86
Figure of an English lady of the
Raj
ivory
Delhi, India
circa 1900-1910
H. 23 cms
Lent by Mr. & Mrs. D. A. Battie

87
Conquistador mask
painted wood
Guatemala
circa mid 20th century
H. 18 cms W. 17 cmg
Lent by the Trustees of The British
Museum, Ethnography Department,
London

88*
Mask
painted wood
Guatemala
circa mid 20th century
H. 18.7 cms W. 16 cms
Lent by the Trustees of The British
Museum, Ethnography Department,
London

89*
Mask representing 'Alvarado'
painted wood
Guatemala
circa mid 20th century
H. 19 cms W. 14.9 cms
Lent by the Trustees of The British
Museum, Ethnography Department,
London

90*
Conquistador mask
painted wood
Guatemala
circa mid 20th century
H. 19 cms W. 16.8 cms
Lent by the Trustees of The British
Museum, Ethnography Department,
London

91*
Español dance mask
painted wood
Guatemala
circa early 20th century
H. 19 cms W. 155 cms
Lent by the Trustees of The British
Museum, Ethnography Department,
London

92
Conquistador mask
painted wood, glass
Ocozocoautla, Chiapas, Mexico
contemporary
H. 16.2 cms
Lent by Chloë Sayer

93
Figure of a horse
Artist: Fidel Navarro
Worn by dancers taking the role of
St. James
painted wood, horse hair
Acapetlahuaya, Guerro, Mexico
contemporary
H. 24 cms
Lent by Chloë Sayer

94
Moros dance mask
painted wood
San Francisco, Guerrero, Mexico
circa 1900s
H. 27 cms W. 16 cms
Lent by the Trustees of The British
Museum, Ethnography Department,
London

95*
Mask representing a French soldier
painted wood
Huejotzingo, Mexico
circa late 19th century
H. 16.2 cms W. 14.5 cms D. 9.5 cms
Lent by The Horniman Museum and
Public Park Trust

96
Viejitos dance mask
gesso and paint on wood
Chaparan, Michoacan, Mexico
circa early 20th century
H. 24.5 cms W. 16 cms
Lent by Royal Pavilion Art gallery
and Museums, Brighton

97
Moros dance mask
Representing 'Señor de Naranja'.
painted wood
Michoacan, Mexico
circa early-mid 20th century
H. 19.5 cms W. 185 cms
Lent by the Trustees of The British
Museum, Ethnography Department,
London

98
**Mask representing a Franciscan
friar**
painted wood
Michoacan-Northeast, Mexico
circa early-mid 20th century
H. 24.5 cms W. 18.5 cms
Lent by the Trustees of The British
Museum, Ethnography Department,
London

99*
Tejorón mask
Representing San Pedro and worn in
the Dance of Tejorones.
painted wood, horse hair and fur
Oaxaca, Mexico
circa early 20th century
H. 17 cms W. 14 cms
Lent by Royal Pavilion Art Gallery
and Museums, Brighton

100
Negritos dance mask
painted wood
Mixteca, Oaxaca, Mexico
circa early 20th century
H. 16.5 cms W. 113 cms
Lent by the Trustees of The British
Museum, Ethnography Department,
London

101
Negritos dance mask
painted wood
Costa Mixteca, Oaxaca, Mexico
circa early-mid 20th century
H. 16.5 cms W. 113 cms
Lent by the Trustees of The British
Museum, Ethnography Department,
London

102*
Dance mask of the Marquez
gesso and paint on wood
Puebla, Mexico
circa early 20th century
H. 20 cms W. 14 cms
Lent by Royal Pavilion Art Gallery
and Museums, Brighton

103*
Moros dance mask
Belonging to a cycle of dances
involving Moors and Christians.
painted wood
Naolinca, Veracruz, Mexico
circa early-mid 20th century
H. 31 cms W. 19 cms
Lent by the Trustees of The British
Museum, Ethnography Department,
London

104*
Moros dance mask
painted wood
Naolinca, Veracruz, Mexico
circa early-mid 20th century
H. 26 cms W. 18.7 cms
Lent by the Trustees of The British
Museum, Ethnography Department,
London

105
Moros dance mask
painted wood
Naolinca, Veracruz, Mexico
circa early-mid 20th century
H. 30 cms W. 18.5 cms
Lent by the Trustees of The British
Museum, Ethnography Department,
London

106
Chonguinada female dance mask
wire mesh, paint, hair, velvet
Chilca, Huancayo, Peru
contemporary
H. 19.5 cms W. 14.5 cms
Lent by the Trustees of The British
Museum, Ethnography Department,
London

107
Chonguinada male dance mask
wire mesh, paint, velvet
Chilca, Huancayo, Peru
contemporary
H. 18.8 cms W. 13 cms
Lent by the Trustees of The British
Museum, Ethnography Department,
London

108
Model cannon currency unit
brass
Brunei, Malaya
L. 27 cms
Lent by the Trustees of The British
Museum, Ethnography Department,
London

109
Newspaper printed on bark cloth
Suva, Fiji Islands
circa 1900
H. 48 cms W. 33.2 cms
Open W. 67.5 cms
Lent by the Trustees of The British
Museum, Ethnography Department,
London

110
Aeroplane shadow puppet
painted leather
Java
L. 38.1 cms
Lent by the Trustees of The British
Museum, Ethnography Department,
London

111
**Bamboo staff, incised, with
depiction of men with axes and a
European with a gun**
New Caledonia
circa 19th century
L. 129.5 cms D. 5.6 cms
Lent by the Trustees of The British
Museum, Ethnography Department,
London

Lenders

Peter Adler, *3, 4, 5, 6, 7, 8, 9, 12, 13*
Mr & Mrs D A Battie, *86*
Royal Pavilion Art Gallery and Museums, Brighton, *21, 37, 38, 39, 96, 99, 102*
City of Bristol Museum and Art Gallery, *16, 56*
Calderdale Museums & Arts, *44, 50, 51*
Sir Hugh Cortazzi, *64, 65*
Durham University Oriental Museum, *67, 68, 69, 70*
Trustees of the National Museums of Scotland, Edinburgh *80*
Eskenazi Ltd, *6*
Michael Graham-Stewart, *11, 20, 30, 33, 40, 41, 42, 43, 46*
The Horniman Museum and Public Park Trust, *29, 32, 95*
India Office Library (British Library), *77, 78, 79, 83, 85*
Ipswich Museums, Ipswich Borough Council, *15, 25, 47, 48, 49, 57*
The Board of Trustees of the National Museums & Galleries on Merseyside, Liverpool Museum, *1, 14, 17, 22, 45, 58, 59, 60*
Manchester Museum, University of Manchester, *19, 28, 34*
Trustees of The British Museum, Ethnography Department, *2, 10, 18, 23, 24, 26, 27, 31, 35, 36, 52, 53, 54, 55, 87, 88, 89, 90, 91, 94, 97, 98, 100, 101, 103, 104, 105, 106, 107, 108, 109, 110, 111*
Chloë Sayer, *92, 93*
Victoria & Albert Museum, *62, 63, 66, 71, 72, 73, 74, 75, 76, 81*
Private Collection *82, 84*

Bibliography

Beier, Ulli, *Art in Nigeria 1960*, Cambridge University Press, 1960

Blackburn, Julia, *The White Men: The First Response of Aboriginal People to the White Man*, Orbis, London, 1979

Brody Esser, Janet, *Faces of Fiesta: Mexican Masks in Context* (Exhibition Catalogue), San Diego State University, San Diego, California, 1981

Brody Esser, Janet, *Behind the Mask in Mexico* (Exhibition Catalogue), Museum of New Mexico Press, Santa Fe, New Mexico, 1988

Burland, Cottie A. *The Exotic White Man: An Alien in Asian and African Art*, photographs by Werner Foreman, Weidenfeld and Nicolson, London, 1969

Carroll, K., *Yoruba Religious Carving*, Geoffrey Chapman, London, 1967

Clifford, J., *The Predicament of Culture*, Harvard Univesity Press, 1988

Cole, H. M., *Mbari: Art and Life Among the Owerri Igbo*, Indiana University Press, Bloomington, 1982

Cole, D., *Captured Heritage: The Scramble for Northwest Coast Artifacts* Douglas & McIntyre, Vancouver and Toronto, 1985

Cordry, Donald B., *Mexican Masks*, University of Texas Press, Austin, Texas, 1980

Clunas, Craig, ed., *Chinese Export Art and Design*, Victoria & Albert Museum, London, 1989

Drew, L. and D. Wilson, *Argillite, Art of the Haida*, Hancock, North Vancouver, 1980

Equiano, Olaudah, *The Life of Olaudah Equiano, or Gustavus Vassa the African*, Longman, 1989

Garlake, P., *Kingdoms of Africa*, Phaidon/Elsevier, Oxford, 1978

León-Portilla, Miguel, *The Broken Spears: The Aztec Account of the Conquest of Mexico*, Beacon Press, Boston, 1966

León-Portilla, Miguel, *El reverso de la Conquista*, Editorial Joaquin Mortiz, Mexico City, 1987

Macnair, P. L. & A. L. Hoover, *The Magic Leaves: A history of Argillite Carving*, British Columbia Provincial Museum, Victoria, 1984

Meech-Pekarik, Julia, *The World of the Meiji Print*, New York & Tokyo, 1986

Mount, Marshall Ward, *African Art: The Years Since 1920*, Indiana University Press, 1973

Picton, J., *Transformations of the artifact: John Wayne, plastic bags, and the Eye-that-Surpasses-All-Other-Eyes*, in C. Deliss, *Lotte or the Transformation of the Object*, Kunstverain Graz, Austria, 1990

Okamoto, Yoshitomo, *The Namban Art of Japan*, New York & Tokyo, 1972

Osborne, Lilly de Jongh, *Indian Crafts of Guatemala and El Salvador*, University of Oklahoma Press, Norman, 1965

Raychaudhuri, Tapan, *Europe Reconsidered, Perceptions of the West in Nineteenth Century Bengal*, Oxford University Press, Delhi, 1988

Sansom, George, *The Western World and Japan*, London, 1950

Sheehan, C., *Pipes That Won't Smoke; Coal That Won't Burn, Haida Sculpture in Argillite*, Glenbow Museum, Calgary

Sullivan, Michael, *The Meeting of Eastern and Western Art*, London, 1973

Tidrick, Kathryn, *Empire and the English Character*, I.B. Tauris, London, 1990

Wescott, J., *The Sculpture and Myths of Eshu-Elegba, Yoruba Trickster*, Africa, XXXII-4, pp336-354, 1962

Notes on the Contributors

Dr Craig Clunas is Deputy Curator of the Far Eastern Collection at the Victoria & Albert Museum

Dr Clémentine Deliss is an anthropologist. She lives and works in London as a free-lance curator, art critic and producer of ethnographic documentaries.

Cyprian Ekwensi is one of Nigeria's foremost novelists. Among his best-known books are *People of the City* and *Jagua Nana*.

Dr Jonathan King is Curator of the North American Collection in the Museum of Mankind.

J.P. Losty is Curator of Prints and Drawings in the British Library (India Office Library and Records).

John Picton is Head of the Department of Art and Archeology and Senior Lecturer in African Art at the School of Oriental and African Studies, London.

Chloë Sayer is the author of several books on Mexico, including *Mexican Textiles* and *The Arts and Crafts of Mexico*. She is a documentary film researcher, and has carried out fieldwork for the Museum of Mankind and contributed to its collections.

Dr Toshio Watanabe is Principal Lecturer in the History of Art and Design at Chelsea College of Art and Design.